D0999529

The American Speller

The American Speller

AN ADAPTATION OF NOAH WEBSTER'S
BLUE-BACKED SPELLER

Illustrated by
BARBARA COONEY

THOMAS Y. CROWELL COMPANY
NEW YORK

By Barbara Cooney

CHANTICLEER AND THE FOX
THE AMERICAN SPELLER

COPYRIGHT © 1960 BY BARBARA COONEY
ALL RIGHTS RESERVED.

NO PART OF THIS BOOK MAY BE REPRODUCED IN ANY FORM, EX-
CEPT BY A REVIEWER, WITHOUT THE PERMISSION OF THE PUB-
LISHER. MANUFACTURED IN THE UNITED STATES OF
AMERICA. LIBRARY OF CONGRESS CATALOG CARD NO. 60-11549

1   2   3   4   5   6   7   8   9   10

A WORD ABOUT THIS BOOK

Several years ago I came across Noah Webster's old Blue-Backed Speller. What a delightful conglomeration of sentences Mr. Webster had assembled to illustrate his spelling rules! They were so full of humor, good sense, information, and vignettes of country life that my mind's eye immediately began planning pictures to accompany them.

Now, having made the pictures, I would like to introduce Noah Webster to the descendants of the millions of Americans who were brought up on his speller. Not only was Noah Webster one of our great teachers, he was also a practical philosopher and an ardent patriot. Indeed, his Blue-Backed Speller, with its pithy sayings, its random bits of information, and its pride in America, played a major part in unifying the newly formed United States. Up and down the eastern seaboard went the little spelling book. As we moved west, across the Alleghenies and to the Rockies, the little book went too. All across our country children were reared with one unified and unifying language and with Noah Webster's homely and attractive precepts in their hearts and minds. Before the speller went out of general usage, almost one hundred million copies of it had been sold. It has been said that, with the exception of the Bible, no book has done more to form the characters and minds of more Americans than this little fourteen-penny spelling book. Like Noah Webster's great dictionary, the Blue-Backed Speller is part of the American heritage.

I hope this book will help, in a pleasant sort of way, to teach children the basic sounds of the American language. There is no short cut to solid learning. Reading is the open sesame to knowledge. If we are to read books, which are made up of sentences, which in turn are made up of words, which in their turn are made up of sounds, then it is reasonable that we should start at the beginning. In this book are presented the essential sounds of our language, presented, I hope, in an enjoyable as well as in a methodical fashion.

Some children may learn something of phonics from this new edition. Others may simply look at the pictures. But many, I hope, will find the words of Noah Webster sticking to their ribs like good roast beef.

Barbara Cooney
Pepperell, Massachusetts
1960

Contents

The American Speller

PART 1

CONSONANTS

B b

Girls are fond of fine beads to wear round their necks.

Bears live in the woods.

Some fishes are very bony.

Bad boys love to rob the nests of birds.

The buffalo has an aversion to fire and to red colors.

Six boys can sit on one long bench.

HARD C c

A cutlass is a broad curving sword.

He had a new red cap.

The cow was in the lot.

A curtain is used to hide something from the view.

4

C c

A citadel is a fortress to defend a city or town.

One dollar is one hundred cents.

Cedar trees grow in the woods.

Cider is made of apples.

The cherry is an acid fruit.

Never go into a barn or stable with a lighted cigar
in your mouth; and it will be better still
if you never have a cigar in your mouth at all.

5

D d

The wild deer runs in the woods.
She can rub off the dust.
The doctor tries to cure the sick.
I can dip the milk with a tin dipper.
Do not sit on the damp ground.
He hid in his den.

F f

The Laplander wraps himself in furs in the winter.

A field requires a good fence to secure the crops.

She has a new fan.

The falcon is a bird of the hawk kind.

Boys like a warm fire on a wintry day.

On the Fourth of July, the bells ring a loud peal.

HARD **G** g

A gander is white and a goose gray.

The good girl may jump the rope.

Shut the gate and keep the hogs out of the yard.

A great gun makes a loud noise.

SOFT G g

The giraffe is a gentle, timid animal living on grass
and shrubs.

H h

The hog inclines to fat.

Doors are hung on hinges.

A boy can harness a horse and hitch him to a wagon.

A holster is a case for carrying a pistol.

The farmer cuts his grass to make hay.

You shall hem and mark all your papa's handkerchiefs.

J j

A jewel is often hung in the ear. Some nations still
wear jewels in the nose.

The little boy likes to have a new jacket.

A toad will jump like a frog.

John Smith, Senior, is father to John Smith, Junior.

K k

Ladies should know how to manage a kitchen.

The kangaroo walks upright, runs fast, and leaps
with astonishing agility.

A kingdom is a country ruled by a king.

L l

We sail for Liverpool tomorrow.

I love the young lady that shows me how to read.

Firemen have ladders to climb up on houses.

A librarian is a person who has charge of a library.

A library is a collection of books.

Lions have long tails.

M m

A monk lives in retirement from the world.

Moss grows on trees in the woods.

Medals are sometimes given as a reward at school.

When it is cold, put your hands in a muff.

N n

Noah and his family outlived all the people who lived
  before the flood.

The farmer eats his dinner at noon.

Neat sewers make handsome seams with their needles.

I had a nut to eat.

The neck must be kept clean.

P p

We poke the fire with a poker.

Never pester the little boys.

I love to eat a good ripe pear.

Hungry boys are apt to eat fast like the pigs.

When we are sick we take pills.

Pocahontas most tenderly entreated the king to let
Captain John Smith live.

Qu qu

Never quarrel with your playmates.

Children should answer questions politely.

Twenty-five cents are equal to one quarter of a dollar.

The porcupine can raise his sharp quills.

Men in old age love a quiet life.

One quart of milk will fill two pint cups.

Quadrupeds are animals which have four feet.

Men make themselves wretched by war and quarrels.

R r

I like to see a full-blown rose.

A rude girl will romp in the street.

When an old house is pulled down it is
   no small job to remove the rubbish.

The rainbow is caused by the sun's shining
   upon the falling rain.

Rabbits hide themselves in secret places.

S s

Ladies wear sashes round the waist.

A good son will help his father.

The sailor steers a vessel with a rudder.

T t

A toothbrush is good to brush your teeth.

She put my cap in the tub.

Teachers teach their pupils, and pupils learn.

A girl can toast a piece of bread.

V
v

Visitors should not make their visits too long.

Women wear veils.

A pastor does not like to see vacant seats in his church.

Men play on the bass viol.

A vain girl is fond of fine things.

Vessels sail on the large rivers.

W w

Children are sometimes bewildered
    and lost in the woods.
Wolves howl in the woods in the night.
Heavy winds sometimes prostrate trees.
Little boys and girls love to ride in a wagon.
Washington was a successful general.

X x

Ann can spin flax.

I met six men today.

Exercise gives relish for food.

The fox is said to be an artful animal.

He stands on a tin box.

Y y

The sheep yields her yearly fleece to furnish us with
warm garments.

The yolk of an egg is yellow.

Put the yoke on the oxen.

Young Washington, that blessed youth, feared God and
loved the truth.

Z z

The zebra is a handsome animal.

The barber shaves his patrons with a razor.

That idle boy is a very lazy fellow.

PART 2

VOWEL SOUNDS

SHORT A a

The first man was Adam, and the first woman was Eve.
The man cuts down trees with his ax.
The little ants make hillocks.
Farmers are sellers of apples and cider.
Hannibal crossed the Alps in the rigor of winter.

LONG A a

Oak trees produce acorns, and little animals eat them.
Girls wear aprons to keep their frocks clean.

ai-ay

We often wait the arrival of the mail.
Friday is just as lucky a day as any other.
The rain runs from the eaves of the house.
You may play on a mow of hay.

SHORT **E** e

The elephant is docile, tractable, and grateful.
A hen will sit on a nest of eggs and hatch chickens.
Sound striking against an object and returned is an echo.
He and she led and fed the deer.

LONG **E** e

Is he to be by me?
She has a new hat.

e a - e e

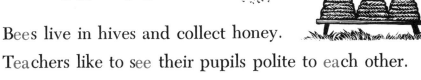

Bees live in hives and collect honey.
Teachers like to see their pupils polite to each other.
We have green peas in the month of June.
Let us rest on the bed, and sleep, if we can.
The peacock is a gaudy, vain, and noisy fowl.

SHORT I i

The Indians give furs for blankets.

The lady instructs her pupils how to spell and read.

Is he to go in?

He is in bed. Let him sit up.

LONG **I** i

Am I to go in?

A forge is a place where iron is hammered.

i e - y

The lark soars into the sky.

We lie down and sleep in beds.

Can a boy cry and not shed a tear?

People pare apples to make pies.

SHORT Oo

It is my ox.
The man can put on his wig.
The otter lives chiefly on fish.
An observatory is a place for

      observing the heavenly bodies with telescopes.

LONG O o

A glade is an opening among trees.

Children should respect and obey their parents.

The potato is a native plant of America.

o a - o e - o w

A roe deer has no horns.

We have snow and ice in the cold winter.

Few men can afford to keep a coach.

SHORT U u

He is to go up.
The sum of four and five is nine.
The moon is much smaller than the sun.
Go up to it.

34

U u

Plows, axes, and hoes are utensils for farming.

The President of the United States is elected once every
four years.

u e - u i

His favorite pie is a blueberry pie.

Glue is made from the hoofs of cattle.

Boys and girls are fond of fruit.

That boy needs a new suit.

PART 3

Special CONSONANT SOUNDS

c h

The boy can chop.

Fill your basket with cherries and give them to your
little friends.

We have heard the chime of church bells.

Children may be helpful to their parents.

We sit in chairs and put our feet on footstools.

...ng

The sting of a wasp is very painful.

In the spring the grass looks fresh and green.

Some ladies are fond of gold rings.

A plum will hang by a stem.

ph

A sphere is a body or globe.

Geography is a description of the earth.

The dolphin is a lucky omen.

37

s h

The sheep have escaped from the pasture.

A shad can swim.

A ship has a tall mast.

Shoemakers drive tacks into the heels of shoes.

t h

A thunderstorm is a sublime scene.

Careless girls mislay their things.

Plants will not thrive among thorns and weeds.

w h

A whale spouts.

Carts, wagons, gigs, and coaches run on wheels.

Whiskers are thought by some to afford protection to
　　　the throat in cold weather.

Never whisper in company.

PART 4

Special VOWEL SOUNDS

SHORT O O

If I meet him in the street, I will greet him with a kind
  look, and show him my new book.

Wool makes the sheep warm.

The good boy will not tear his book.

A wild boar lives in the woods.

LONG O O

Boys sometimes get upon the roof of a shed
    and leap into the snow.
He that lies in bed when he should go to school
    is not wise.
Carrots have long tapering roots.
Men inflate balloons with gas, which is
    lighter than common air.

41

a u - a w

A saucy stubborn child displeases his parents.
Cranberry sauce tastes good with roast turkey.
Children bawl for trifles.
The bull bellows and paws the ground.

o u - o w

The owl has large eyes and can see in the night. The
female owl makes her nest in an old hollow tree,
or among the cliffs of the mountain, or in an old
deserted house or a castle.

oi - oy

When you can choose for yourself, try to make a good choice.

Boys love to make a great racket.

A pin has a sharp point.

Hard shells incase clams and oysters.

PART 5

SILENT LETTERS

SILENT b

Boys should not climb over fences to get fruit which is
    not their own.

Look to the gentle lambs.

We move our limbs at the joints.

Get up, Charles. Wash your hands, comb your hair, and
    get ready for breakfast.

SILENT C

Needles and scissors are utensils for making garments

SILENT g

The writer sometimes signs his name.

SILENT k

When good boys and girls are at church they will sit,
  kneel or stand still.
Knead the dough thoroughly, if you would have
  good bread.
The little sister can knit a pair of garters.

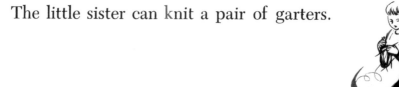

SILENT g h

The bright stars without number adorn the skies.

Smoke rises, because it is lighter than the air.

You should visit your neighbor who is sick.

With blankets or buffalo skins persons may ride in a
sleigh with comfort in the coldest weather.

SILENT t

On Christmas day people express to each other their
     good wishes, and little boys and girls expect gifts
     of little books, toys and plums.
A moat is a deep trench around a castle.
Tents are fastened with stakes.

48

SILENT **W**

Children make wry faces when they eat sour grapes.
Washerwomen wring clothes.
That girl's bonnet is awry.
Men wrapped in wool and fur prepare to meet the
 chilling blast.

PART 6

VOWELS FOLLOWED BY *r*

er-ir-ur

Turks wore turbans instead of hats.

She put her hat on the bed.

A bird flew over the house.

Parents deserve the kind treatment of children.

Little girls love to play with dolls and babies.

The fur of the beaver makes the best hats.

Puss likes to sit on your lap and purr.

a r

William Tell was an expert archer.

The new table stands in the parlor.

Gardens are sometimes surrounded by a fence
made of pales.

o r

A portrait is a picture bearing the likeness of a person.

The horse drinks at the pump.

The mason puts a layer of mortar between bricks.

PART 7

CONSONANT BLENDS

b r

Bridges are made across rivers.

Ladies sometimes wear bracelets on their arms.

c r

The little boys can crack nuts with a hammer.

Snakes creep.

A king and queen may wear crowns of gold.

Crows pull up and eat corn.

d r

The boy had a drum.

You must keep your dress neat and clean.

A dromedary is a large quadruped.

f r

To frounce is to curl or frizzle, as the hair.

Little boys and girls must not be fretful.

Will you help me pin my frock?

We like to have our friends visit us.

g r

Gravestones are placed by graves.

I will wear my greatcoat on a cold wet day.

I like to play in the shady grove.

A grotto is a cavern or cave.

The color of the wolf's eye is a fiery green.

p r

A proboscis is a long tube or snout from the mouth
 or jaw.

The preacher is to preach the gospel.

A prodigy is something very wonderful.

Parents protect and instruct their children.

s h r

When the cock crows, he makes a shrill loud noise.

t h r

Saul threw his javelin at David.

t r

The ladies adorn their heads and necks with tresses.
Leave off your bad tricks.
He set a trap for a rat.
A trout is a good fish to eat.

s c

To prevent the crow's ravages, the farmers erect
  scarecrows.
If you go too near a hot fire it may singe or scorch
  your frock.

s p

Spiders spin webs to catch flies.
Always listen when you are spoken to, and never
  interrupt the speaker.

s t

I like to see a good stone wall around a farm.
The horns of the stag are shed every year between
        February and May and replaced with new ones.
Never hold anybody by the button or hand in order
        to be heard through your story.
Do not let children stare at strangers.

scr

A cross cat will scratch with her sharp nails.
A postscript is something added to a letter.

spr

People admire the beautiful flowers of spring.

s t r

We should be attentive and helpful to strangers.
One boy must not strike another, nor push him down,
   nor throw stones at him. This is wrong
   and mean.
See William picking strawberries. Bring him a basket.
   Let him put the berries in a basket and
   carry them to his mama and sisters.

b l

The old sheep bleats, and calls her lamb to her.
Blackberries and raspberries grow on briers.
We see a fine blush on the cheek.

c l

Grapes grow on vines, in clusters.

The weaver makes cloth on a loom.

An ox loves to eat clover.

A clown makes us laugh.

f l

He that lies down with dogs must rise up with fleas.
Among the Alps is seen the shepherd with his pipe con-
ducting his flock.

g l

Glass is made fast in the window with putty.
He was glad to see me.

p l

A duck is a plump fowl.

I had some ice cream on a plate in July.

s l

My good little sister may have a slate and pencil,

   and she may make letters on her slate.

A boy can ride on a sled.

s k

The boy that skates must have many a fall.

Try to be a skillful workman.

A skiff is a small rowboat.

s m

A smile shows that we are pleased.

Something in the kitchen smells good.

s n

Boys love to play and roll about in snow. And when
the snow is moist, the young rogues will make
snowballs and throw them at each other.
Never snatch a book from anyone.

s w

The smell of the pink is sweet.
A swamp is wet, spongy land.

s q u

A squirrel will climb a tree quicker than a boy.
The gray and black squirrels live in the forest and
make a nest of leaves and sticks on the high
branches. They subsist on nuts, which they
hold in their paws, using them as little boys
use their hands.

d w

I dwell in a new brick house.

t w

Twelve o'clock at night is midnight.
Twelve months make a year.
Twelve things make a dozen.

PART 8

WORDS ENDING IN *le*

72

...le

The eagle lives in solitude.

Your little fingers are very handy with the needle.

The place where the bell hangs in the steeple is called
the belfry.

A pony is a very little horse.

The Holy Bible is the book of God.

The little girl sets her doll in a little chair beside a table
furnished with teacups as big as a thimble.

A little boy can drive the cows to pasture.

WORDS CONTAINING *ci*, *si*, *ti*

ci

A tiger has great strength, and is very ferocious.
The turtle is deemed a delicious dish.

si

A mansion is a place of residence, or dwelling.
Anger is a tormenting passion.
Love is an agreeable passion.

ti

Savage nations inhabit huts and wigwams.
A dog is a most affectionate and faithful animal.

PART 10

WORDS ENDING IN *e*

. . . e

King David rode upon a mule.
Sick people look pale.
He came in haste, and left his book.
A dime is a small coin worth ten cents.
I will kiss the babe on his cheek.
Sometimes we have cakes.
We love to hear a fine tune.
I hope to hop the rope.

Noah Webster

Noah Webster was born in West Hartford, Connecticut, on October 16, 1758. The son of a Yankee farmer, he was not brought up to be idle. Like other farmers' sons, he rose early, milked the cows and drove them to pasture, hitched the team, plowed the fields, mended stone walls, chopped wood, and, when he could, attended classes in the local log school. In 1774 his father sent him off to Yale College with the admonition to "serve your generation and do good in the world." Here his studies were interrupted by a short stint in the Revolutionary Army. Upon his graduation from Yale in 1778 he became a schoolteacher. It was during this period that he became aware of the disorderly schools and the poor textbooks they used. In 1783 he published his Blue-Backed Speller, the first in a series of improved schoolbooks. In 1789 he married Rebecca Greenleaf of Boston. They had two sons and six daughters.

Noah Webster studied and practiced law; campaigned successfully for copyright legislation; served as a judge, as a member of both the Connecticut and the Massachusetts legislatures, and in other public offices; became a lecturer and literary critic; edited a magazine and two newspapers; wrote a number of other books and pamphlets; and assisted in the founding of Amherst College, where he was the first president of its board of trustees. In 1828, at the age of seventy and after twenty years of preparation, he published his great American dictionary. Five years later his American revised version of the Bible was published. He died in New Haven, Connecticut, on May 28, 1843, at the age of eighty-four.

Barbara Cooney

Barbara Cooney has drawn pictures all her life. Born in Brooklyn, New York, she spent her summers in Waldoboro, Maine. Here her mother painted for fun, and this started young Barbara off. Her interest in art became serious as she continued her schooling at Great Neck Country Day School and then at Briarcliff School. At Smith, art was her major; later she studied etching and lithography at the Art Students' League in New York City.

In 1949 Miss Cooney married Dr. C. Talbot Porter, a general practitioner, and settled in a rambling sixteen-room house in Pepperell, Massachusetts. This home is shared with their four children, a poodle, and assorted cats. An avid interest in gardening is in evidence from early spring through late fall when blossoms and herbs flourish in the Porters' garden.

In 1959 Miss Cooney received the Caldecott Medal for *Chanticleer and the Fox*. This medal is given by the American Library Association for the most distinguished picture book of the year. Her work in *The American Speller* marks a handsome addition to the long list of books she has illustrated.